First published by

Copyright by Anas
Illustrations by An

Design by Anastasia Sichkarenko

Distributed by:
Turnaround Publisher Services Ltd.
Unit 3
Olympia Trading Estate
London N2Z 6TZ

T: +44 (0)20 8829 3019

ISBN 0-9548- 213-8

Anastasia Sichkarenko is a Graphic Designer and Illustrator
who lives and works in London. Borne in Ukraine just at the
end of the Communist Regime she now looks back at it with a
humour and irony.

ANASTASIA'S
VERY LARGE
COMMUNISM
HANDBOOK

POCKET
HEDGEHOGS

Communism, it would be true to say, has had quite an impact on the twentieth century (and actually the nineteenth and twenty-first as well).

It would also be true to say that it's pretty much had it's fifteen minutes of fame, or perhaps it was slightly longer, but anyway it's looking fairly out of fashion, except in China where it's be- come a slightly odd Confucian capitalist Communism. There's a few communists left in Nepal and other places but in the West it's about as popular as parking wardens, with whom it has a certain resonance.

So why was communism such a big deal, and what did it mean? In this little book we'll answer some of these ques- tions by quoting what various thinkers have had to say on the issue. This is al- ways a good way of looking at the prob- lem because one good quote is worth

100 pages of propaganda. That's probably why Mao had a little red book of quotes so that everyone could remember what the point was.

"YOU CANNOT REDUCE THE COMPLEX TO THE SIMPLE, ONLY THE OTHER WAY AROUND." KARL RIBEROV.

Perhaps Communism was a brilliant idea that only nasty human nature messed up, or perhaps it was a really nasty idea that only real human nature put a stop to. Either way it was definitely something of an issue, and that's what this book is all about.

Philosophers have only interpreted the world the point is to misunderstand it. Communism may well have been the ultimate expression of a crazy philosophical rationalism that thought it could reduce everything to a kind of logic, the trouble is, people aren't thinking machines.

COMMUNISM IS LIKE PURITY, IT'S A FINE IDEA BUT TEMPTATION CONSTANTLY GETS IN THE WAY. EYE

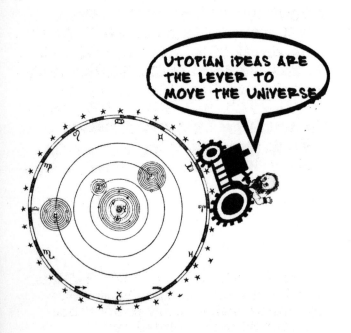

ORIGINS.

FROM A "PRAGMATIC" POINT
OF VIEW, POLITICAL PHILOSOPHY
IS A MONSTER AND WHENEVER
IT HAS BEEN TAKEN SERIOUSLY,
THE CONSEQUENCE, ALMOST
INVARIABLY, HAS BEEN REVOLU-
TION, WAR, AND EVENTUALLY,
THE POLICE STATE.
HENRY DAVID.

The philosophers have only interpreted
the world in various ways the point is to
change it.
Marx.

There is a debate about whether Jesus
was the first communist, but the Rus-
sian nineteenth-century philosopher
Vladimir Soloviev pointed out:
Jesus urged his followers to give up
their own possessions whereas socialists
and communists want to give away the
possessions of others.

Socialism is the same as Communism,
only better English.
George Bernard Shaw

Q)What is Socialism?
A)The longest possible way to communism.

WHAT IS COMMUNISM REALLY?

Trotsky described the transformation of mankind after the communist revolution:
Man will, at last, begin to harmonize himself in earnest...He will want to master first the semi-conscious and then also the unconscious processes of his own organism: breathing, the circulation of blood, digestion, and, within the necessary limits, subordinate them to the control of reason and will...

Arthur Koestler compared joining the Communist Party with religious conversion:
To say that one had `seen the light` is a poor description of the mental rapture which only one convert knows...There is now an answer to every question, doubts and conflicts are a matter of the tortured past.

Religion is opium for the masses.
Marx

ARE COMMUNISTS CRAZY?

i AM NOT A MARXIST.
KARL MARX

Capital is dead labor, which, vampire-like, lives only by sucking living labor, and lives the more, the more labor it sucks.
Marx

Psychiatry also has something to say about the mental state of the Communist followers.

I have no concern with any economic criticisms of the communist system; I cannot inquire into whether the abolition of private property is expedient or advantageous. But I am able to recognize that the psychological premises on which the system is based are an untenable illusion. In abolishing private property we deprive the human love of aggression of one of its instruments... but we have in no way altered the differences in power and influence which are misused by aggressiveness.
Sigmund Freud

Communism is not love. Communism is a hammer which we use to crush the enemy.
Mao-Tsi-Tung

...I believed passionately that Communists were a race of horned men who divided their time equally between the burning of Nancy Drew books and the devising of a plan of nuclear attack that would land the largest and most lethal bomb squarely upon the third-grade class of Thomas Jefferson School in Morristown, New Jersey.
Fran Lebowitz.

Communists are people who fancied that they had an unhappy childhood.
Gertrude Stein

Positivists accept, and indeed enlarge, the programme of Communism; but we reject its practical solution...
The ignorance of the true laws of social life under which Communists labour is evident in their dangerous tendency to suppress individuality.
Etieene Condillac.

A SPECTER IS HAUNTING EUROPE
THE SPECTER OF COMMUNISM.
MARX.

HOW TO MAKE REVOLUTIONS.

Thinkers prepare the revolution and bandits carry it out.
Azuela Mariano

Revolution is an abrupt change in the form of misgovernment.
Bience Ambrose

"First, I want to let you know that I came to join the revolution, not to kill the Cambodian people,"
Pol Pot

It is impossible to predict the time and progress of revolution. It is governed by its own more or less mysterious laws.
Vladimir Lenin

The first duty of the revolutionary is to get away with it.
Abbie Hoffman

The most radical revolutionary will become a conservative the day after the revolution.
Hannah Arendt

A modern revolutionary group heads for the television station.
Abbie Hoffman

Those who have served the cause of the revolution have ploughed the sea.
Simón Bolívar

Never wear your best trousers when you go out to fight for freedom and truth.
Henric Ibsen

LOOKS LIKE THOSE BOURGEOISIE INTELLECTUALS ARE AT IT AGAIN

A revolution is not a bed of roses. A revolution is a struggle to the death between the future and the past.
Fidel Castro

Every revolution evaporates and leaves behind only the slime of a new bureaucracy.
Franz Kafka

Revolution, in order to be creative, cannot do without either a moral or metaphysical rule to balance the insanity of history.
Camus Albert

One revolution is just like one cocktail;
it just gets you organized for the next.
Will Rogers.

IT IS DIFFICULT TO TELL
WHETHER REVOLUTIONS
IMPROVE THINGS

Without a revolutionary theory there
cannot be a revolutionary movement.
 Vladimir Lenin

A revolution is not a dinner party, or
writing an essay, or painting a picture,
or doing embroidery; it cannot be so
refined, so leisurely and gentle, so tem-
perate, kind, courteous, restrained and
magnanimous. A revolution is an insur-
rection, an act of violence by which one
class overthrows another.
Mao Tse-Tung

Revolutions are not made for export.
Khrushchev

It is the good children, Madame, who make the most terrible revolutionaries. They say nothing, they do not hide under the table, they eat only one sweet at a time, but later on, they make Society pay dearly for it!
Jaun-Paul Sartre.

HOW CAN YOU MAKE A REVOLUTION WITHOUT EXECUTIONS?
LENIN

In a revolution, as in a novel. the most difficult part to invent is the end.
Alexis de Tocqueville

Revolutions always come round again.
That's why they're called revolutions.
Terry Pratchett

CHE iS DEAD! GET OVER iT!

THE RUSSIAN REVOLUTION.

Revolution was supposed to happen in the industrialized countries but the first big one was in semi-feudal Russia

The workers themselves constituted at best 2 or 3 percent of Russia population as the industry was yet to catch up with the industrial revolution in the West. And only about 5 percent of those workers belonged to the communist party in pre-Revolutionary Russia

I am patriot for Russia, the Future is there. Russia will win out and it will save the world. That is my belief. But I don't want to live there.
Lincoln Steffenson

Lenin's Bolshevik party claimed to represent the working class, however only one solitary worker ever sat on the executive board of Lenin's party, and he turned out to be a police spy.

In November 1917 we knew that our victory will be a lasting victory only when our undertaking will conquer the whole world, because we had launched it exclusively counting on the world revolution.
Lenin

Krispin pointed out: it is only worth to starting a revolution if it will not diminish the living conditions of the working class.

To which Lenin replied:

When we will organize dictatorship some workers will starve and their living conditions will be greatly reduced, but the victory of communism couldn't be achieved without some sacrifice from the working class.

Sociological Questionnaire after the revolution.
-Where were you bourn?
-In Saint Petersburg.
-Where did you go to school?
-In Petrograd.
-Where do you live now?
-In Leningrad.
-Where would you like to live?
-In Saint Petersburg.

Workers of the world unite, you have nothing to loose but your chains.
Marx

So they united, and the Communist revolution took the chain from their legs and wound it around their necks.
Samuel Bonom

The policy of Russia is changeless. Its methods, its tactics, its maneuvers may change, but the polar star of its policy, world domination, is a fixed star.
 Marx

HERE IS A CHILD OF BOLSHEVIC REVOLUTION!

We are heading in the right direction, comrades!
Lenin.

 The slanders poured down like Niagara. If you take into consideration the setting—the war and the revolution—and the character of the accused—revolutionary leaders of millions who were conducting their party to the sovereign power—you can say without exaggeration that July 1917 was the month of the most gigantic slander in world history.
Trotsky

BY THE WAY ABOUT BOLSHEVISM:
ONE HAS TO REMEMBER THAT
ALL THAT IS PUBLISHED IN THE
PRESS IS PROPAGANDA, THAT THE
BOLSHEVIKI ARE THE MODERATE
SOCIAL-REVOLUTIONARIES, A PO-
LITICAL PARTY, AND THE SOVIETS
ARE A SYSTEM OF GOVERNMENT
BASED ON THE IDEA OF "PURE
DEMOCRACY" THAT EVERY MAN
SHALL TAKE DIRECT PART IN THE
GOVERNMENT OF THE COUNTRY
JHON DOS PASSOS

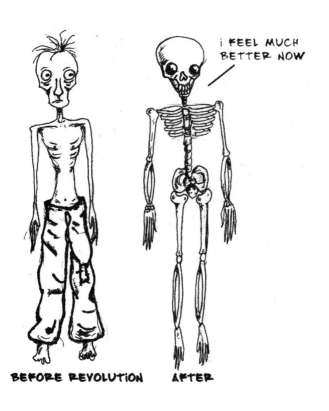

LENIN AND STALIN

Lenin defined "dictatorship of the proletariat" as power that is limited by nothing, by no laws, that is restrained by
absolutely no rules, that rest directly on
coercion. Commenting on famine in the
Volga region Lenin said that it is pro-
gressive as it destroys old peasant econ-
omy and paved the way for socialism.

Others loved themselves, money, theo-
ries, power: Lenin loved his fellow
men.... Lenin was God, as Christ was
God, because God is Love and Christ and
Lenin were all Love
Isidora Duncan

Morality serves to destroy dictatorship of the old regime, and to unite all workers within the proletariat that will create new communist society.
Lenin

Lenin resented my opposition in the name of revolutionary justice. So I called in exasperation, `Then why do we bother with a Commissariat of Justice? Let's call it frankly the Commissariat for Social Extermination and be done with it!` Lenin's face suddenly brightened and he replied, `Well put...that's exactly what it should be...but we can't say that.
Leon Trotsky.

The Capitalists will sell us the rope with
which we will hang them.
Lenin

**COMMUNISM IS SOVIET GOVERN-
MENT PLUS THE ELECTRIFICATION
OF THE WHOLE COUNTRY.
LENIN**

STALINIST PURGES
ARE LOT'S OF
FUN

It is precisely now and only now, when in the starving regions people are eating human flesh, and hundreds if not thousands of corpses are littering the roads, that we can (and therefore must) carry out the confiscation of church valuables with the most savage and merciless energy... so as to secure for ourselves a fund of several hundred gold rubels.
Lenin

Vyacheslav Molotov, when asked who was more ruthless Stalin or Lenin, replied:
Lenin, of course...I recall how he scolded Stalin for softness and liberalism.

GOOD OLD JOE

(Dont forget he was our ally
in the second World War)

Crisis alone permitted the authorities to
demand-and obtain-total submission and
all necessary sacrifices from its citizens.
Stalin

A single death is a tragedy; a million
deaths is a statistic.
Stalin.

The people who cast the votes don't de-
cide an election, the people who count
the votes do.
Stalin.

Ideas are fare more powerful than guns.
We don't allow our enemies to have
guns, why should we allow them to have
ideas?
Stalin.

The great thing about prison camps is that they create loads of jobs!

EVERY ONE IN THE SOVIET UNION HAS A JOB!

In the Soviet army it takes more courage
to retreat than to advance.
Stalin.

**DEATH SOLVES ALL PROBLEMS –
NO MAN, NO PROBLEM.
JOSEPH STALIN**

No chronology of Soviet atrocities can convey the crushing of the human spirit under Lenin and his successors. But the retelling of 70 years of grisly facts leaves little doubt that what we face today in Soviet communism is, indeed, an 'evil empire'.
Michael Johns

AFTER THE SECOND WORLD WAR
WE REMEMBERED THAT STALIN
WAS A DANGEROUS LUNATIC, SO
WE STARTED THE...

COLD WAR

FROM STETTIN IN THE BALTIC TO TRIESTE IN THE ADRIATIC, AN IRON CURTAIN HAS DESCENDED ACROSS THE CONTINENT.
WINSTON CHURCHILL.

The general population of the Soviet Union was fairly ignorant of the country's foreign policy, the Vietnam war caused no protests or demonstrations; and in 1953 Great Soviet Encyclopedia described Mahatma Gandhi as an agent of British imperialism.

MAO AND THE COLD WAR

War is the highest form of struggle for resolving contradictions`; `Political power grows out of the barrel of the gun`.
Mao Tse-Dong.

If the worst came to worst and half of the mankind died, the other half would remain while imperialism would be razed to the ground and the whole world would become socialist.
Mao Tse-Dong.

CASTRO AND THE COLD WAR

Moscow was at first cautious in supporting Cuban leader Fidel Castro for fear of USA reaction but Castro's skilful politics ensured Soviet help as they nursed a dream of having an island of socialism in the Atlantic ocean.

During the Cuban Missile Crisis, Castro had urged Moscow to launch a preemptive nuclear strike against the United States, being prepared to sacrifice Cuba in order to assure the worldwide triumph of `socialism`.

The revolution needs the enemy... revolution needs for its development its antithesis, which is counterrevolution.
Fidel Castro

YES THERE IS LIFE ON MARS BUT PLEASE DON'T TELL COMRAD KHRUSCHEV, OTHER-WISE HE MAY TRY TO TURN THEM COMMUNIST
CCCP
CCCP
CCCP

With his trademark courage and conviction, President Reagan led us out of the Cold War, spreading his vision of freedom, resulting in the release of millions of people from the yoke of communism.
John T. Doolittle

We helped keep the Cold War cold. . .
.A war without casualties cannot be as famous as a horrible war, but it is preferable.
Edward Teller.

KHRUSCHEV AND THE COLD WAR

About the capitalists states, it doesn't depend on you whether we (Soviet Union) exist. If you don't like us, don't accept our invitations and don't invite us to come to see you. Whether you like it or not history is on our side. We will bury you.
Nikita Khruschev

I once said "We will bury you" and got in to trouble with it. Of course we will not bury you with a shovel. Your own working class will bury you.
Nikita Khruschev.

BERLIN IS A TESTICLE OF THE
WEST. WHEN I WANT THE WEST
TO SCREAM I, SQUEEZE ON BER-
LIN.
NIKITA KHRUSCHEV.

NiXON AND COLD WAR

The Cold War isn't thawing; it is burning with a deadly heat. Communism
isn't sleeping; it is, as always, plotting,
scheming, working, fighting.
Richard M Nixon.

The communists have lost the cold war,
but the west has not yet won it.
Nixon

A man may die, nations may rise and fall, but an idea lives on. Ideas have endurance without death.
John F. Kennedy

For us in Russia communism is a dead dog. For many people in the West, it is still a living lion.
Alexander Solzhenitsyn.

COMMUNISM LIKE RELIGION IS A WONDERFUL IDEA IN THEORY, ITS JUST THAT THE PRACTICE IS ALWAYS CARRIED OUT BY HUMANS NOT ANGELS.

WHY DOESNT iT WORK?

Why doesn't Communism work? Is it because people aren't suited for its great utopian ideas or is it because people who in charge of the Communist states care only about fulfilling their own utopia. As Mikhail Bakunin said: "Powerful states can maintain themselves only by crime, little states are virtuous only by weakness." Or as Karl Popper said: "Philosophers should consider the fact that the greatest happiness principle can easily be made an excuse for a benevolent dictatorship."

Under capitalism man exploits man. Under communism it's just the opposite. John Kenneth Galbriath.

You'll see certain Pythagoreans whose belief in communism of property goes to such lengths that they pick up anything lying about unguarded, and make off with it without a qualm of conscience as if it had come to them by law.
Erasmus Desiderius.

In a country where the sole employer is the state, opposition means slow starvation. The old principle, who does not work shall not eat, has been replaced by a new one: who does not obey shall not eat.
Leon Trotsky

All fingers are not alike, if you cut the bigger ones to make all equal it is communism. If you stretch the smaller ones to make all equal its socialism. If you do nothing to make all equal its capitalism.
B J Gupta.

In our country the lie has become not just a moral category but a pillar of the State.
Alexander Solzhenitsyn.

Throw a theory into the fire; it only spoils life.
Mikhail Bakunin.

The Catholic and the Communist are alike in assuming that an opponent cannot be both honest and intelligent.
George Orwell.

Under communism (socialism), there is no incentive to supply people with anything they need or want, including safety.
George Reisman

Communism works on paper but never works on people.
José Reyes

55

You can talk about capitalism and communism and all that sort of thing, but the important thing is the struggle everybody is engaged in to get better living conditions, and they are not interested too much in government.
Bernard Baruch

It was characteristic of the rise of the Nazi movement in Germany and of the Communist movements in Europe after 1930 that they recruited their members from this mass of apparently indifferent people whom all other parties had given up as too apathetic or too stupid for their attention.
Hanah Arendit

COMMUNISM DOESN'T WORK BE-
CAUSE PEOPLE LIKE TO OWN
STUFF.
FRANK ZAPPA.

We were all witnessing the formation of a new system of production, of government, and of exploitation of man by man, which was and is neither capitalist nor socialist; a system which needs to be labeled with a new term and which, without going deeply into a debate over terminology, can only be called Totalitarian. The novelty, vigour and cruelty of this system goes far beyond the most pessimistic predictions of the most bitter and lucid members of the Opposition. Victor Serge.

COMMUNIST JOKES

Q)Which two systems cannot coexist?
A)Socialist and nervous.

Lenin proved that people can rule the country, Stalin proved that one man can rule the country, Khrushchev proved that any one can rule the country. Breshnev proved that nobody needs to rule the country.

Six paradoxes of socialism: no one works, but the plan is met; plan is met, but nothing gets produced; nothing gets produced, but everyone's refrigerators are full; refrigerates are full, but everyone complains; everyone complains, but nobody protests; nobody protests, but prisons are filled up.

Apart from their other characteristics, the outstanding thing about China's 600 million people is that they are `poor and blank.`
Mao Zeodong.

MY LARGE PRINT MAO'S RED BOOK IS A BIT DIFFICULT TO BE EXCITED ABOUT!

I don't like Communism because it hands out wealth through rationing books.
Omar Torrijos Herrera

A worker may be the hammer's master, but the hammer still prevails. A tool knows exactly how it is meant to be handled, while the user of the tool can only have an approximate idea.
Milan Kundera.

Good tests kill flawed theories; we remain alive to guess again.
Karl Popper

If we had more time for discussion we should probably have made a great many more mistakes.
Leon Trotsky.

WHAT'S HAPPENING NOW.

Blow the dust off the clock. Your watch-
es are behind the times. Throw open the
heavy curtains which are so dear to you
-- you do not even suspect that the day
has already dawned outside.
Alexander Solzhenitsyn.

DEMOCRACY WAS BEING SAVED FROM COMMUNISM BY GETTING RID OF DEMOCRACY.
JUAN BOSCH

The war against terror is every bit as
important as our fight against fascism
in World War II. Or our struggle against
the spread of Communism during the
Cold War.
Jim Bunning

Let's not talk about Communism. Communism was just an idea, just pie in the
sky.
Boris Yeltsin.

We first fought the heathens in the name of religion, then Communism, and now in the name of drugs and terrorism. Our excuses for global domination always change.
Serj Tankian

In today's world, our freedoms are being monkeyed with. The same way McCarthy ignited the fear of communism, politicians are igniting the fear of terrorism and using it for political ends.
John Mellencamp

We found not the passionate mobs going forward under new flags to struggles begun anew each day in tragic and fruitful confusions, but a sort of vast administration, an army, a machine in which the most burning energies and the clearest intelligences were coldly integrated and which performed its task inexorably.
Victor Serge.

GORBACHEV AND NEW WORLD ORDER

I'm a Communist, a convinced Communist! For some that may be a fantasy. But to me it is my main goal.
Mikhail Gorbachev.

The soviet people want full-blooded and unconditional democracy.
Gorbachev.

The market came with the dawn of civilization and it is not an invention of capitalism. If it leads to improving the well-being of the people there is no contradiction with socialism.
Gorbachev.

In the end we beat them with Levi 501 jeans. Seventy-two years of Communist indoctrination and propaganda was drowned out by a three-ounce Sony Walkman. A huge totalitarian system has been brought to its knees because nobody wants to wear Bulgarian shoes. Now they're lunch, and we're number one on the planet.
O'Rourke.

A LOT OF MY FRIENDS ARE TROTSKYISTS

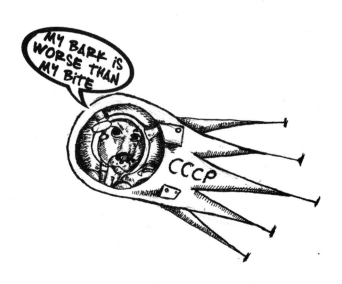

THE LEGACY

We will teach the sun and the moon to change places. We shall create a new heaven and earth for man.
Mao Zeodong.

The Black Book of Communism ... In Mao's China, the communists didn't eat babies, but they boiled them to fertilize the fields.
Silviano Berlusconi

I believe, as Lenin said, that this revolutionary chaos may yet crystallize into new forms of life.
Mikhail Gorbachev.

Lenin

If you look at the mirror it appears that Lenin was pointing in to the other direction.

My Homer is not a communist. He may be a liar, a pig, an idiot, a communist, but he is not a porn star.
The Simpsons.

How do you tell a communist? Well, it's someone who reads Marx and Lenin. And how do you tell an anti-Communist? It's someone who understands Marx and Lenin.
Ronald Reagan.

High culture is nothing but a child of that European perversion called history, the obsession we have with going forward, with considering the sequence of generations a relay race in which everyone surpasses his predecessor . . .
Milan Kundera.

OPTIMISM IS OPIUM FOR THE PEOPLE.
MILAN KUNDERA.

Civilization has made the peasantry its pack animal. The bourgeoisie in the long run only changed the form of the pack.
Leon Trotsky.

Comrades! We must abolish the cult of the individual decisively, once and for all.
Nikita Khruschev.

Get back to work you lazy bastards

Communism continued to haunt Europe as a specter - a name men gave to their own fears and blunders. But the crusade against Communism was even more imaginary than the specter of Communism. A. J. P. Taylor.

In the Soviet Union, capitalism triumphed over communism. In this country, capitalism triumphed over democracy.
Fran Lebowitz

It would have been difficult to design a
path out of communism worse than the
one that has been followed.
Aleksandr Solzhenitsyn

We were sent to Vietnam to kill Communism. But we found instead that we were killing women and children.
John F. Kerry

When I die, my only wish is that Cambodia remain Cambodia and belong to the West. It is over for communism, and I want to stress that.
Pol Pot

I still call myself a communist, because communism is no more what Russia made of it than Christianity is what the churches make of it. But if by some freak of history communism had caught up with this country, I would have been one of the first people thrown in jail.
Pete Seeger

THE IDEA OF COMMUNISM ISN'T WORTH MUCH IN THEORY.